FUNKdrumming
Innovative Grooves & Advanced Concepts

By MIKE CLARK
Transcribed by Towner Galaher

Recorded and mixed at Bedford Studio by Andy Tommasi
Mastered by Thom Camuso

PLAYBACK+
Speed · Pitch · Balance · Loop

To access audio visit:
www.halleonard.com/mylibrary

6438-0872-0879-2529

T0033991

ISBN 978-0-634-07975-7

HAL•LEONARD®

Visit Hal Leonard Online at
www.halleonard.com

Contact us:
Hal Leonard
7777 West Bluemound Road
Milwaukee, WI 53213
Email: info@halleonard.com

In Europe, contact:
Hal Leonard Europe Limited
42 Wigmore Street
Marylebone, London, W1U 2RN
Email: info@halleonardeurope.com

In Australia, contact:
Hal Leonard Australia Pty. Ltd.
4 Lentara Court
Cheltenham, Victoria, 3192 Australia
Email: info@halleonard.com.au

Dedication

This book is dedicated to Ray Torres, my teacher, my friend, and my inspiration. He is one of the funkiest drummers on the planet and a man of immense humanity.

Table of Contents

Biography

"He's a great jazz drummer, and he hasn't lost any of the stuff that he brought from Oakland. So now he's totally free to do both, and he does. The solo he played on the album *Thrust*, on the song "Actual Proof," is one of the best drum solos on any of my albums. So many people have remarked about that solo, saying, 'Incredible.'"

–Herbie Hancock

Mike Clark gained worldwide recognition as one of America's foremost jazz and funk drummers while playing with Herbie Hancock's group in the early 1970s. Mike became known as a major innovator through his incisive playing on Hancock's *Thrust* album, which garnered him an international cult following.

Mike has performed and recorded with jazz greats such as Herbie Hancock, Chet Baker, Tony Bennett, Wayne Shorter, Joe Henderson, Bobby Hutcherson, Woody Shaw, Pharoah Sanders, Vince Guaraldi, Cal Tjader, Harold Land, Wallace Roney, Chris Potter, Kenny Baron, Buster Williams, Eddie Henderson, Nat Adderly, Fred Wesley, Oscar Brown Jr., Mose Allison, Bobby McFerrin, Larry Coryell, Mulgrew Miller, James Williams, Geri Allen, Billy Childs, Michael Wolff, Onaje Allan Gumbs, John Abercrombie, Dave Liebman, Jack Walrath, Jack Wilkins, James Genus, Bob Hurst, Bootsy Collins, Al Jarreau, Big Nick Nicholas, Clarence "Gatemouth" Brown, Otis Rush, Big Jay McNeely, Ray Sharpe, Jimmy Reed, Albert King, Albert Collins, Jack McDuff, Delbert McClinton, Brian Auger and the Oblivion Express, Bill Doggett, Maxine Brown, Gil Evans and his orchestra, and Brand X, the acclaimed British fusion band. He has performed throughout the world at all the major jazz festivals.

A faculty member of Drummers Collective, Mike has appeared at college clinics throughout the world and has been featured in *Downbeat, Musician, International Musician & Recording World, Modern Drummer, Jazz Times, Guitar Player, Jazz Is,* and many jazz history and method books.

Often referred to as "one of the most sampled drummers in hip hop," Mike's beats have been used on tracks by musicians as diverse as NWA, Grandmaster Flash, Britney Spears, Janet Jackson, Christina Aguilera, Prince, and many others.

His numerous recording credits include albums with Herbie Hancock, the Headhunters, Brand X, Eddie Henderson, Jack Walrath, Jack Wilkins, Mark Puricelli, Mike Wolff, and Alien Army, a group led by guitar great Jack Wilkins. As a bandleader, his release *Give the Drummer Some* was very enthusiastically received, earning a rare four and a half stars in *Downbeat*, as was *The Funk Stops Here*, a joint effort with Hancock alumnus Paul Jackson. In 2001, Mike released his very popular solo album *Actual Proof*. His most recent acoustic jazz endeavor, *Summertime*, featuring Chris Potter and Billy Childs, was released in February of 2003 to favorable reviews and spent several weeks in the Top Ten charts.

Several recent efforts have included a compilation of his legendary, innovative funk beat samples, *Mike Clark—The Headhunter*, a re-release of the widely acclaimed *Thrust* album, and in 1998, *The Return of the Headhunters*, featuring Herbie Hancock. Next came *Herbie Hancock's Box Set*, featuring Headhunter classics "Actual Proof" and "Butterfly" from *Thrust*, a few choice cuts from *Manchild*, and also some historical tracks from the classic *Flood*, previously only available in Japan.

His band Prescription Renewal, which debuted in the winter of 2000, electrified audiences across the country with an eclectic core of cross-generational multi-talents such as Charlie Hunter, Fred Wesley, Skerik, Robert Walter, and DJ Logic. They also frequently featured stellar special guests such as George Porter, Jr. of Funky Meters fame, Kyle Hollingsworth of the String Cheese Incident, Les Claypool, Will Bernard, Rob Wasserman, Larry Goldings, Reuben Wilson, and fellow Headhunters alumnus Bill Summers, becoming a big hit on the thriving young jam band scene. Touring concurrently that year and the next were the Roots Funk All Stars, another hot act that married Mike with James Brown trombonist Fred Wesley, former Headhunter cohort and funk bassist legend Paul Jackson, Dr. Lonnie Smith, and Robben Ford.

His latest projects include the Headhunters' newest effort, *Evolution/Revolution*. This new Headhunter configuration, with original founding members Mike, Bill Summers, and Paul Jackson, is augmented by Donald Harrison, Victor Atkins (Los Hombres Caliente), and Nicholas Payton.

Mike recently toured and recorded with piano great Michael Wolff and his band, Impure Thoughts. 2003 has also seen Mike touring with the Headhunters, Prescription Renewal, the Roots Funk All Stars, and his own band, featuring the music of *Summertime*. His work continues to influence yet a new generation of drummers, as it always has, since his sensational arrival on the music scene with Herbie Hancock and the Headhunters.

Mike is also very excited about his recent venture with fellow drummer Lenny White, New Brew, which debuted at B.B. King's in New York in the summer of 2004, featuring Stanley Clarke, Victor Bailey, Robben Ford, Kenny Garrett, Eddie Henderson, George Colligan, and DJ Logic.

Talk About the Funk

An Interview with Mike Clark

Towner Galaher: Who were some of your early musical influences, as far as drummers go?

Mike Clark: As far as drummers go, my father was listening to records with Gene Krupa, Big Sid Catlett, Baby Dodds, Zutty Singleton, Jo Jones, Buddy Rich, and Louis Bellson. Those were some of the first guys that I heard. And even before that, I listened to records that—I didn't know who the drummers were. We also had what they now call jump records, like Louis Jordan and that type of thing. I was listening to those records, not knowing the drummers' names. I also heard records by Count Basie, Duke Ellington, Benny Goodman, Louis Armstrong, Louis Prima, Jack Teagarden, Jonah Jones—all kinds of jazz cats. My dad was also a boogie woogie and blues head, so I was hearing Roy Brown, Phil Harris, Will Bradley and Wynonie Harris, Louis Jordan, and guys who played like that.

T.G.: Do you think you internalized much of what you heard and assimilated it into your style?

M.C.: Yeah, completely, because I listened to those guys all day, every day for years. Then one day he brought home a record—I think it was *Son of Drum Suite*—and I heard Art Blakey for the first time, and that's when I became interested in bebop. I instinctively understood and loved it straight away. From there I found Charlie Parker and everybody since concerning bebop.

T.G.: That's interesting. I was also initially drawn into bebop through an encounter with Art Blakey.

M.C.: I hear you. I couldn't believe the impact of his ride beat. I'd never thought about music in those terms before. It captivated me, and in fact, to this day, I'm still mesmerized by that type of thing. Blakey had such a deep feel for swing. Well, that led me to Max Roach and then soon after, Roy Haynes and Philly Joe Jones. (I really got into Philly a few years later; I started to understand his poetry.) And that led me to Elvin Jones, Tony Williams, Lenny White, and so forth.

T.G.: Can you relay a couple of powerful turning points—a certain record you heard or live performance that had a big impact on your drumming?

M.C.: I saw a lot of live drummers, but they weren't all name drummers. In those days, most clubs had jazz bands, so I saw a lot of live jazz being played. I remember some of the first drummers I met were Dick Johnson, who played with trumpet players Mike Lala and Murphy Campo at the Famous Door in New Orleans, and another guy named Paul Ferrara, who played with Al Hirt and Louis Prima. I saw many drummers throughout Texas in jazz clubs, but I can't remember who they were. My dad took me to all these places when I was seven or eight years old. These guys weren't famous drummers; in those days there were a lot of working jazz bands. I later saw Buddy Rich and Louis Bellson live. There was a swing club in Fort Worth where they would play.

T.G.: I used to take lessons at a local drum shop in Portland, Oregon, where I grew up, and one day Sonny Payne came in and sat down at a set of drums in the front room and went off. I vividly remember thinking, incredible! I had never seen anyone play like that before, and it opened my eyes to what was possible on a set of drums.

M.C.: It's a good thing you mentioned Sonny Payne. He could really play! When I was twelve or thirteen, I was in California, and I used to go see Sonny Payne in Sacramento at the Memorial Auditorium with Count Basie. Also, Rufus Speedy Jones, and a little later, Sam Woodyard, who both played with Duke Ellington. By then, I was getting into clubs and went with my dad to see Max, Philly Joe, the drummers of the day. So, by that time, I had seen and heard everybody, except for Elvin Jones and Tony Williams—just about everybody we know about from that time period in jazz. Yeah, they all influenced me—each one of them.

T.G.: Fast forward to your teenage years. Who were you listening to then?

M.C.: Well, the same guys—and I'm still listening to those guys now—with a few new additions. James Brown had come out with some hits, and I was involved in a lot of so-called "soul bands" during that time. So, by then, I was going to hear the Ike & Tina Turner Revue, James Brown, Hank Ballard, Bobby Blue Bland, and any kind of soul music or rhythm and blues experience that I could have. I was influenced by Tina Turner's drummer. I don't recall his name, but I remember he had a set of blue WFL drums. I met him, and he taught me how to tune my snare tight so it would crack through a big auditorium. I'd go see James Brown and check out his drummers. I'm not sure who they were, but it was in 1961 or 1962.

Me playing at the Famous Door in New Orleans with trumpeter Murphy Campo at age eleven. The guy standing next to me could very well be a young Dr. John.

T.G.: What struck you most about those soul and R&B drummers?

M.C.: I'd never heard the bass drum syncopated and punctuated like that before, and their snare drums would really crack and snap. The backbeats were often displaced—they weren't always on two and four, and I found it as interesting and as soulful as jazz. It hit me hard right away and still does.

T.G.: You dug the intensity and energy of that music?

M.C.: Yeah, well, also, it was my high school music that we were listening to when you'd go on a date or when you'd go to a party and hang out with your friends.

T.G.: So it was your social environment.

M.C.: Indeed. And because I was a good drummer at that time, I could translate those beats very fast. I started getting called to gigs like that, so whatever cover bands were around that were playing that kind of stuff, I was getting the calls to do so. So, at an early age, I got a lot of experience playing the funky stuff.

T.G.: And you played blues and organ trios as well?

M.C.: That came a little later. By the time I was sixteen or seventeen, I had played several organ gigs. I had already started getting blues gigs when I was fourteen. You could work in clubs in those days, and nobody said anything about it. Especially in the south, nobody cared.

They just wanted a drummer. So I'd been involved in R&B and blues from around the time I was fourteen. And these were not just one-nighters. These gigs would last for weeks, months, or sometimes, years. Jazz drummers sounded suspect when they played funk in those days. They had the wrong sound and couldn't coordinate the beats.

I was playing professionally, so I got experience—not just listening to records or working out beats, but logging in air miles on the bandstand.

T.G.: How about big bands?

M.C.: I played in several big bands when I was eight or nine years old. I was featured as a child drum prodigy on a television show so I would have a drum feature. I played in a junior high and high school band and in some union hall rehearsal big bands as well.

I was a guest soloist in the Paul Neighbors Big Band at the Blue Room in the Roosevelt Hotel in New Orleans also at age eleven.

T.G.: Ok, now let's fast forward again to the three- or four-year period prior to when you got the gig with Herbie. What kind of music were you playing then, and who were you listening to most intently during that time?

M.C.: I played jazz gigs and tons of chitlin' circuit organ gigs. That's where I developed the sixteenth-note thing. We played jazz almost all night and inevitably we'd play a few boogaloo tunes. The standard boogaloo beats were too square for me, or so I thought at the time, being young and thinking I was bad.

T.G.: So you spiced them up.

M.C.: So I spiced 'em up, just to avoid boredom, because in those days we were working five nights a week, four or more sets a night. Also, I had my own organ trio, and although we played jazz, because of the nature of the beast, we'd eventually play something funky. Nobody called it funk back then or used words like "pocket" or any of that. People would just say, "play something funky."

Outside of that, I was working mostly acoustic jazz gigs in the Bay Area. Funk was just something you had to know to make a living, and I enjoyed it. You had to play all kinds of music to work, so it became part of my experience.

T.G.: When you landed the gig with Herbie, you found yourself involved in pioneering a new style of music that included incorporating the drumming styles developed by Elvin Jones and Tony Williams into a new idiom that was centered on a sixteenth- and straight-eighth feel. How did you and Paul Jackson and Herbie and that band develop this new rhythmic style?

M.C.: Well, Paul and I had been playing together for years in many bands before we got with Herbie. Whenever we played funk gigs, we immediately gravitated toward that style as a natural expression. It just came out. It was a kind of telepathy we had developed as a result of, and as an expression of our friendship. I mean, we would just start doing that stuff, and then we would start crackin' up because it felt so good! We just kept on doing it. We got very popular around the Bay Area for playing like that and became an in-demand rhythm section for just about anyone who was into that kind of thing.

So, when I was at the audition with Herbie, Paul and I started playing like that right away, and it blew Herbie's mind. He loved it, and we could see that he was having a blast. He responded by coming up with something right there on the spot that went right with it. We didn't discuss anything; it was spontaneous, in the mentality or spirit of the jazz tradition.

T.G.: Many rhythm sections tend to find a one-, two-, or four-bar pattern and pretty much stick with it throughout the tune, but with you guys the ideas would continue to evolve, displacing the beat, changing the syncopation, extending it over a very long section of the tune or sometimes over the entire song.

M.C.: Yeah. It was like I heard Elvin Jones playing over the bar and over the bar and over the bar for days, so we tried to do the same thing. Although it was a different rhythmic structure, we applied the same concept. We'd explore the solos the same way as our predecessors did, playing polyrhythms, over the bar line phrasing, and extending the ideas. Herbie, Paul, and I were hearing everything all the time—like dogs can hear a thunderstorm from miles away. We were reacting to each other from moment to moment. It was amazing.

If you simply play one pattern over and over it becomes like a backdrop for a soloist, devoid of interaction, whereas we were constantly having a group dialogue, reacting and interacting.

I was forever listening to John Coltrane and Miles Davis, so it was about improvisation and listening to everything all of the time. I have carried that spirit on to this day in my approach to music.

T.G.: During that time period, it became quite popular to play in odd time signatures, which you guys certainly did. What I also noticed is that in addition to that, you made great use of hemiolas, the playing of odd rhythmic groupings or phrasing such as fives or sevens and so forth, superimposed over 4/4, crossing over the bar line for extended parts of the tune. These may give the impression that one is playing in an odd time signature while the tune might still be in 4/4.

M.C.: It was kind of a natural extension of the time period, musically, what was going on. Right before the Headhunters, Herbie had the band Mwandishi, and they were making wide use of both odd time signatures and hemiolas, so my thought was why not use some of that to start and finish phrases—not just drum phrases, but as a part of the tune itself. So we'd take a section, and it would appear to be in a different time signature, but it was an odd phrase that, like you said, was superimposed over 4/4. And we did stuff in odd times as well. Sometimes we'd get so far into it that we'd be way out on a limb and then be looking at each other, wondering how, and if, it was going to be resolved.

Sometimes we would just experiment with adding or subtracting beats and finding a way for it to work out. We found a lot of different ways to approach that. There was a lot of experimentation taking place, and also I was picking this stuff up through osmosis from Hancock. He already had those types of things under control. Just by comping for him and listening to his solos, I learned through absorbing his ideas.

Me with my best friend and lifelong bandmate, the incredible bassist Paul Jackson.

T.G.: So, these ideas came from the premier jazz groups of the sixties: Coltrane and Miles. Listening to the records you made with Herbie, I also sense that you achieved another of the prime elements of those two groups: the development of a very high level of telepathic communication. This also played a key role in that group's musical makeup.

M.C.: Yeah, it was the same type of thing applied to a new idiom.

T.G.: Let's talk about your personal musical philosophy. You have tremendous chops and technical ability, but you never seem to make these an end. Rather, you utilize these most effectively as a means for self-expression. Also, through your experiences, you have come to realize how to play the types of things that will be most effective and meaningful—things that will strike a chord in the hearts and minds of the musicians you are playing with, and the audience as well.

M.C.: I play the drums totally for the sake of the music—not for the sake of the drums. I'm constantly striving to carry on an improvised conversation with anyone who is receptive. I listen intensely to everyone and am responding to what I am hearing. It's a natural way for me to play. I don't approach it from the point of "hey, look what I can do!" or for the sake of show, etc. I hope the hallmark of a great drummer has not come to how many fast rolls he can play around the drum set. If that's the case, the music and the feeling will suffer deeply.

T.G.: One prominent aspect of your playing is the use of ghost notes, often using triplets, with the left hand taking the second and third note of the triplet. What, in your opinion, does this add to the music?

M.C.: Well, I think it adds a totally funky feel to the music because you create an undercurrent that's happening at all times. To me, it feels like somebody is shaking a tambourine, or in other words, an undercurrent of events where there is a smaller picture going on inside the big picture, so that you have another layer of sound to listen to or feel. I developed it because of my jazz background where the left would be chattering all the time, talking to the soloist, so for me it was a natural thing. I didn't even think about it; I just did it. I didn't even call them ghost notes in those days—it was just a part of the vernacular and a sign of the times. I mean, first you had Clyde Stubblefield, Bernard Purdie, then soon after, myself, David Garibaldi, Gaylord Birch—that generation of drummers had kind of, I would say, come to that conclusion—a logical extension, based on what had preceded it. It seemed destined to go there, anyway. The guys that were credited with that type of innovation, I think, had arrived there as a natural expression of what time it was politically, musically—just the climate of our country at that time as well as the evolution of rhythm at that point. The music always reflects what the people are feeling and going through. I think we all owe Clyde Stubblefield, Jabo Starks, and Bernard Purdie a deep debt of gratitude.

You notice that each generation of drummers takes the previous generations' inventions and ups the ante or raises the bar. Techniques improve, everything improves (hopefully), as the years go by. I was of that generation, whereas the guys before me played more simply than we did. We were hearing what they did, and armed with youthful enthusiasm, we built further on what they had done. Our stuff was on the cutting edge of the time.

T.G.: Let's talk about Oakland. You mentioned the drummer for Cold Blood, Gaylord Birch. Dave Garibaldi with Tower of Power comes to mind, and, of course, you and Paul were there. What was happening around Oakland at that time that gave birth to what came to be known as the "Oakland sound?"

M.C.: We were all working in small clubs. None of us, at that point, were well known or had established big careers or reputations, but we were working every night. That seemed to be the logical conclusion of the place the new music was going to go, as far as funky music was concerned. In that particular area, we all seemed to be interested in that type of sound. And going from club to club, you'd hear that kind of rhythm, and it was both exciting and new. It became like a war cry for Oakland. Whenever you heard those kinds of beats, Oakland was the first thing you would think of—even back to before Tower of Power or the Headhunters had any records out. I'm talking about two or three years before that happened.

Tony Williams had turned everybody on to a new style of drumming. You had to play funky or commercial music to stay alive at that point, but after listening to Tony Williams all day, those types of inventions, based on what we thought he was doing, started showing up in the music. We practiced those types of things all day. It was really exciting; it was like wearing a badge, or like a club we belonged to. It was our banner. It signified that you were from Oakland and you were funky and this is where you were coming from. Everyone gave us respect as soon as they heard what we were doing. Even some very famous older drummers would come to my gigs and hear me play and tell me they had no idea of how we were putting it together.

T.G.: Describe the social climate. What was going on and how did it reflect in the music?

M.C.: It was right during and after the Huey Newton/Black Panther thing. Black consciousness was just coming to the forefront of America. Oakland had a lot of violence, there was a lot of energy, and, of course, the Hippie movement was in full swing. The war protests were going on, and people were getting hip to what was happening in our country. There was a lot of anger, frustration, betrayal, and hurt. So, naturally, as a result of all that, there was a lot of energy and music coming out of the Bay Area that was very inventive. It was a very exciting time. I've never seen anything like it, to this day, and I've been all over the world.

T.G.: There was a lot of intensity?

M.C.: A lot of intensity. It was on twenty-four hours a day.

T.G.: And that spawned a lot of creativity?

M.C.: Yeah, because people were opening their eyes to what was going on with the government—the lies being fed to the people about what was really happening. The truth about the oppression of African Americans and other minorities, all of a sudden, as they say, consciousness was being raised. Prior to that, it was the Eisenhower generation, where most people thought America was perfect, and then all of the sudden, boom! The Vietnam War came on and stirred up strong feelings among the people, and all that surfaced and manifested a very creative realm. We experienced and lived these events as part of our daily life, and our music was a natural expression and reflection of what was in the air. Everybody was trying to break the chain of the past and open up their lives. It was really an exciting and exhilarating time to be part of, and also a very creative time for all kinds of music and all kinds of people. The Bay Area produced a multitude of great rock, funk, soul, and jazz groups.

Opening Groove

Track 1 "Syncopated Insanity"

Note from the Author

Track 2

Most of the transcriptions in this book represent the first two, four, eight, or sixteen measures of a given song. It is important to note that this drumming style is deeply immersed in a jazz background, which is based on experimentation and variations. Therefore, as you listen to the original recordings you will find that these grooves quickly evolve wherever the imagination leads. The accents shift, and the beats change, resulting in infinite variations.

I have always played original grooves as well as ideas based on the historical roots of jazz, blues, and R&B. I have written many of them for you in this book. After mastering these grooves, I encourage you to move on and create your own. Use your own bass drum patterns, snare accents, and hi-hat parts. I would hope that you don't simply copy what I have come up with, but instead use it as a springboard to create your own individual ideas and fresh concepts—your own "talking drum," so to speak.

Legend

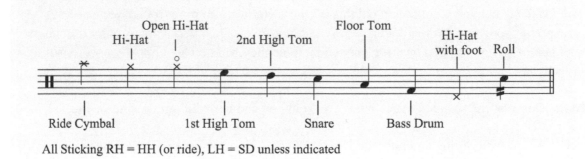

All Sticking RH = HH (or ride), LH = SD unless indicated

The Backbeat

To me, the backbeat is the meat and potatoes of funk drumming. It is the single most important beat of the groove; it is the final statement of where the time lays. As much as I love syncopation, slick rhythms, broken hi-hats, snare patterns, polyrhythmic phrasing and feel, without a fat backbeat, it doesn't mean a thing. A strong backbeat is the hook that all else hangs on. That said, I will try to explain how to get a good backbeat, or as many of the great blues artists used to yell, "Put some bacon fat on it!"

At the moment of impact when the stick hits the snare, I always sort of push or mash down on the drumstick for about a nanosecond, leaving the stick on the head just a little longer than one might think necessary. I use the shoulder of the stick to get a good rim shot. The shoulder strikes the rim simultaneously as the tip hits the center of the drumhead. This avoids getting a nasal "dang" sound and gets a sort of "shtaack!" sound. This creates a fat, strong backbeat where the pendulum stops and starts swinging back the other way.

12

One-Measure Grooves

These are some of my favorite one-measure grooves. Most of these are my originals, based on what I have heard the great masters before me play. I always try to make them interesting, as well as funky, so they will draw in the listener as well as my fellow musicians. Always try to be original and fresh. I wrote this book to get you thinking along those lines.

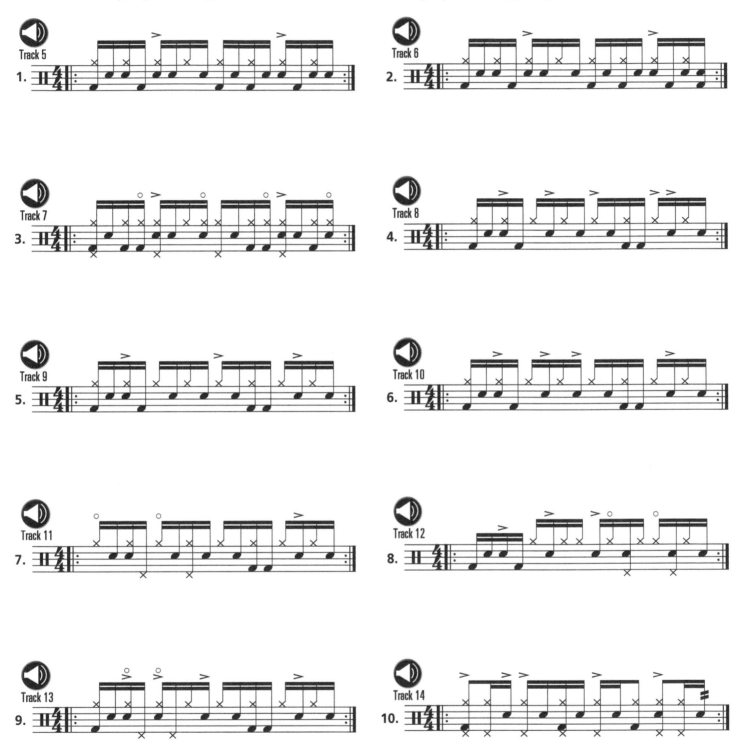

11.

12.

13.

14.

15.

16.

17.

18.

Variations on Groove 18

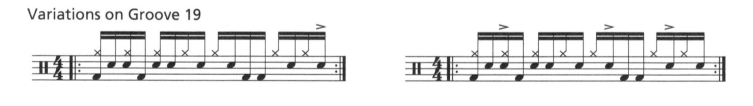

19.

Variations on Groove 19

Two-Measure Grooves

T.G.: Rhythms that are built on two-measure phrases have a natural framework that provides a balance of push and pull, tension and release, call and response. This is the hallmark of all Afro-Caribbean music, centering on the clave rhythm. I know that many Latin drummers have remarked that your funk grooves are very much in clave. In Jack DeJohnette's book *The Art of Jazz Drumming*, he cites "Actual Proof" as an example of a jazz-funk tune that is clave-based. I once played some of your one-measure grooves for Kenwood Dennard, and his first comment was that they sounded very West African. I'm sure you've heard these types of comments many times.

M.C.: I hear that a lot, and actually, although I hadn't studied those idioms per se, I was steeped in the traditions of blues, rhythm and blues, and jazz. Since all of that music traces its ancestry back to Africa, I'm not surprised that the roots are showing, so to speak.

7.

L R L R R L L R R

8.

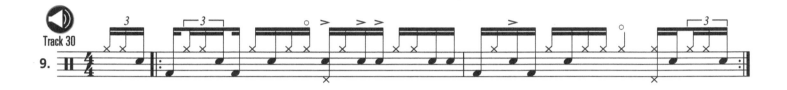

9.

10.

11.

L L R L R R

12.

13.

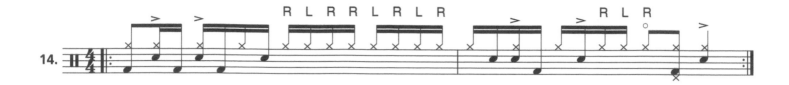

14.

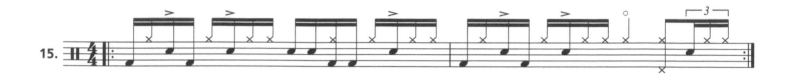

15.

16.

17.

18.

19.

20.

Linear Grooves

I started playing like this in the early seventies. I got tired of being chained to the independence and unisons of hands and feet. I wanted a looser, more transparent sound and lighter feel to the rhythm—not as thick as what most drummers were doing at the time. To accomplish this, I started striking the instruments one at a time with different limbs. (Note: Mike is considered one of the pioneers of this kind of drumming.) After mastering these examples, make up your own. It's fun.

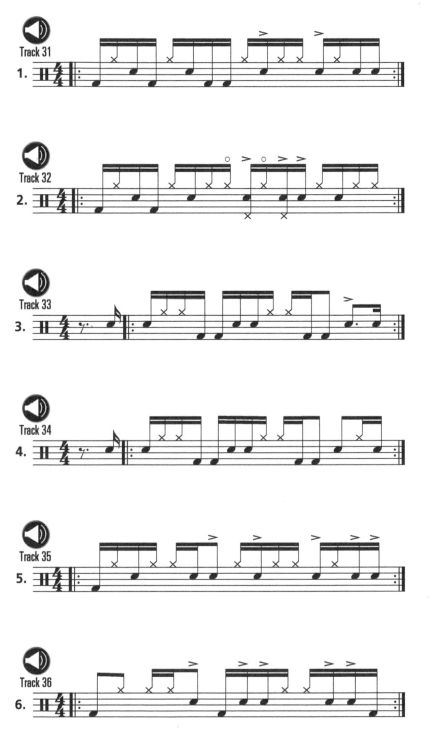

8.

9.

10.

11.

12.

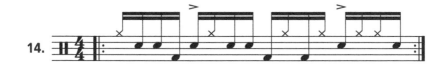

13.

14.

15.

16.

17.

Reverse Hands

I started developing the linear grooves with the hands reversed—left hand on the hi-hat, right hand on the snare—because at one point I wanted a stronger backbeat that I could sink in deeper and figured I could hit harder with my right hand. I soon discovered this wasn't necessarily true, but it was a challenge to play with the hands reversed. I found this challenge attractive, so I pushed myself to keep experimenting with the technique.

I started with paradiddles and then continued to venture out from there. The further I got into it, the more fun I had. It freed me up to do a host of other things, and I discovered all kinds of new ideas, such as getting to the ride cymbal with the right hand without interfering with the time. It also forced me to play with a somewhat different feel that I enjoyed as well. It felt a bit looser playing this way because I was less adept at it. Experiment with this technique and see what you can come up with. Here are a few of my favorites.

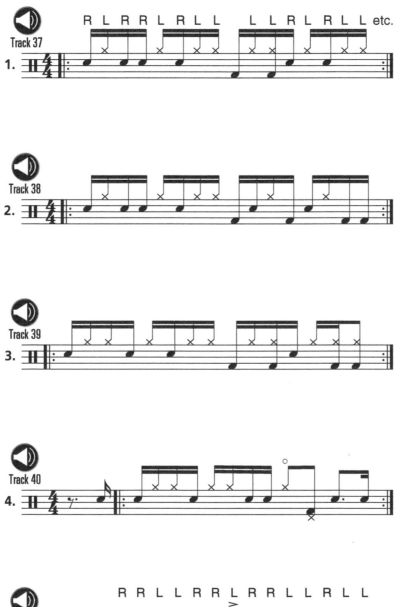

6.

7.

8.

9.

10.

11.

12.

13.

14.

15.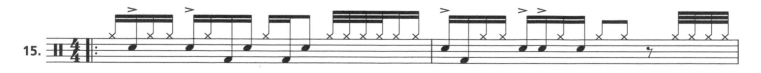

Styles and Variations

Swingin' Funk

Many of the current hip-hop tracks use a kind of swinging-type funk groove. I have used these kinds of grooves since high school. They seem to have been forgotten until recently. You have to play sort of a swing feel on the hi-hat or ride cymbal while maintaining a funk type of backbeat groove underneath. If you swing it too wide it will sound corny, and if you straighten it out too much it won't swing at all. Jabo Starks was a master of this type of groove. You can hear him play like this on many James Brown tunes such as "Sex Machine" and "Make It Funky."

The objective is to get the "swingin' funk" somewhere between straight sixteenths and sixteenth-note triplets. You often hear this referred to as "playing in the crack." Since there is no way of notating this, I have written the examples in straight sixteenths. You will have to bend the straight sixteenths toward a triplet. Listen to the recorded examples to get the right feel. Also check out some New Orleans music and drumming for some excellent examples of really funky rhythms being bent between triplets and straight eighths or straight sixteenths.

Jabo Starks "Love Lights"

Here's another classic Jabo Starks beat. He played with Bobby Blue Bland in the sixties and later went with James Brown. Bobby Blue Bland had a hit called "Turn on Your Love Lights," and it was a challenge to us when we were young to play that beat. So being that it was part of my roots, part of my training was to master that beat. As time went on, I found more modern and up-to-date ways to make it work for me.

It is also recommended to use an eighth-note hi-hat pattern or mix it with the written pattern.

Track 49
1.

Track 50
2.

Track 51
3.

Track 52
4.

Track 53
5.

Track 54
6.

The Breakdown

I created this beat with the idea in mind of something like the feel on "Bitches Brew." I wanted a bottom-ended feeling where the bass drum was carrying the weight of the rhythm—a rhythmical understanding that doesn't require a backbeat—in other words, keeping the funk in it with the foot providing all the syncopation. The hands are just coasting over the top like an idling engine.

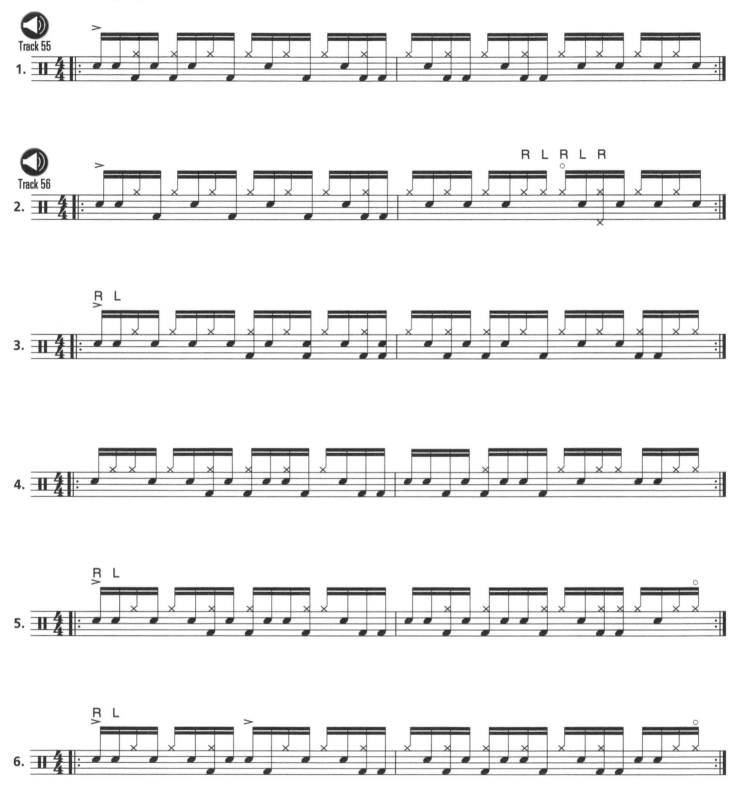

Track 57

Elvin Jones Triplet Style

Elvin Jones used triplets unlike anyone I've heard. Rather than simply using them as an ornament to dress up a beat, he would imbed them within the beat itself, propelling the music forward. When playing in this style, I like to drag the left hand the way Elvin does (as do jazz drummers), with the back half of the triplet in between the backbeats. Through my understanding of the jazz language, I punctuate with the bass drum and left hand.

Basic Hand Pattern:

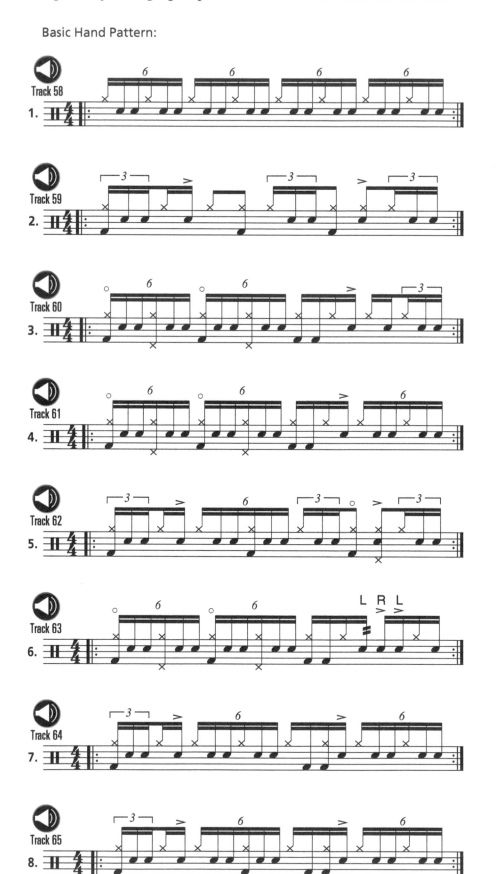

Lenny White "Red Clay"

For those of us who love James Brown, Miles Davis, and John Coltrane, "Red Clay" was our war cry. This was the first time I had heard real jazz and real funk combined. Lenny's beat on "Red Clay" is one of the all-time classics. The groove is real loose and funky, yet real loose and jazzy. Lenny's music is informed by the past, while he plays in the present with his eye on the future. I know this for a fact because I play with him in our new band New Brew.

Basic Pattern:

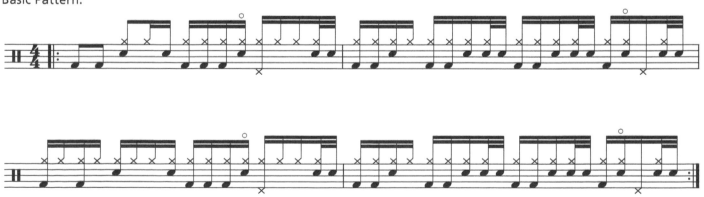

Ride Cymbal Funk

In these examples we're incorporating the ride cymbal for a different flavor. Notice how it helps the groove to open up and breathe a bit more. This can provide a nice boost of energy underneath a soloist.

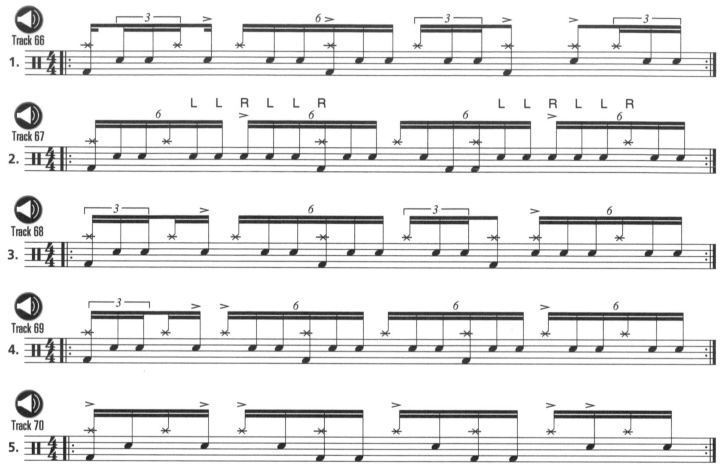

Ride Cymbal Funk with Floor Tom

M.C.: I started using the floor tom as a part of the beat when I got with the Headhunters in 1973 because the band was loud and I wanted a really strong sound for the rhythm. During the solos when the band was really wide open, the snare drum's high pitch would have trouble cutting through, so I started using the floor tom. It not only cut through, it created a really primal sound, and I dug it. I've been using it a lot again recently with Prescription Renewal and have modernized it further.

The floor tom is great in a loud situation. It communicates to the audiences a great sense of rhythmic propulsion.

T.G.: You mentioned that this type of beat is great for propelling a soloist.

M.C.: Yeah, exactly, because if the soloist decides to take it to a certain feverish pitch, sometimes you need something more powerful than the high pitch of the snare drum. The floor tom creates a different color. It's a fatter sound that broadens out the spectrum of the music. A good example of this is on a tune named "Slinky," where Kenny Garrett and I really get into it. It's on my album *The Funk Stops Here* (Enja).

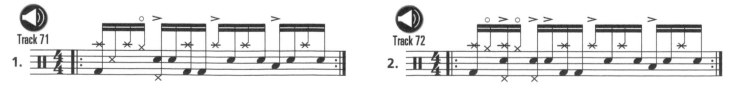

Latin Funk

Here is some Latin funk where I use either son clave or rumba clave on the snare. I use different tom tom patterns to create another dimension or layer to the groove. Please feel free to invent your own snare and tom patterns. It is also a good idea to develop the coordination to be able to improvise with the left hand against the cymbal, tom, and bass drum patterns.

RH = cymbal & tom toms
LH = SD

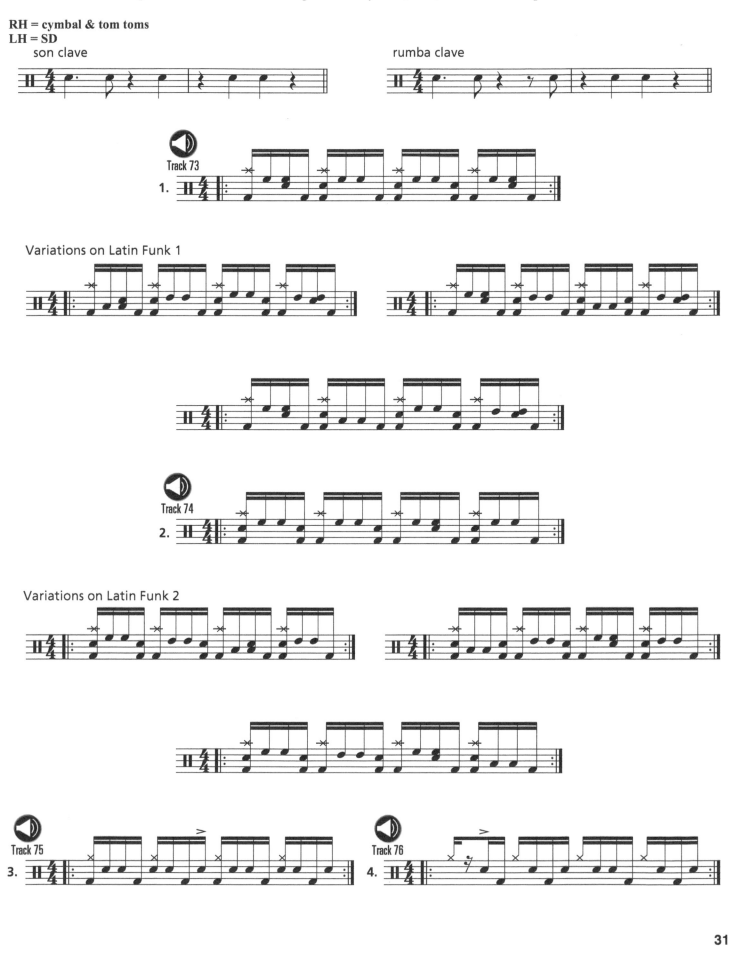

The Shuffle

T.G.: As advanced as young drummers have become, many have overlooked the art of how to play a great shuffle. Let's show them some of your classic shuffles and discuss the hows and whys of this infectious rhythm.

M.C.: All right. The first one here is the double shuffle. I usually play straight four on the bass drum with occasional variations. I hit the backbeat really solid and then I dig the stick in a little bit after I hit it to create a wide swinging feel. I play this particular shuffle wide open. It's not tight and clean.

T.G.: How does this affect the music?

M.C.: Well, it really opens it up. It makes it swing really hard—a really obvious shuffle. This is how the blues guys used to play before the influence of rock. It was almost like a jazz gig in those days.

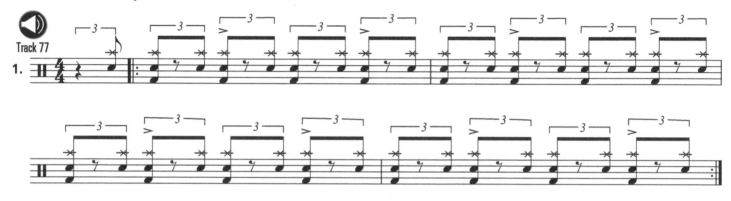

T.G.: That brings us to the next point. There's a time when you play the same shuffle where the pendulum is swung to the opposite side—where you do play it tight.

M.C.: That's right. This one swings and cooks, too. The idea is, as you said, to play it tight where the ride beat is closer to a dotted eighth/sixteenth feel. This is a traditional shuffle that I'd hear guys play around Texas a long time ago. Sonny Freeman, B.B. King's drummer, played this shuffle at times. Check out *B.B. King Live at the Regal*.

As you said, sometimes you play a shuffle and you put the swing notes really together and tight—the extreme opposite of the previous one. You're putting an extreme amount of heat on each note, cutting each note off tight. It creates a feeling like a galloping horse. It swings like crazy in its own way.

Taste and experience will dictate which type of shuffle will create the desired effect for a particular song.

T.G.: I would ask you about the next one and what it does, but I know very well from my own experience.

M.C.: Yeah, exactly. The old blues cats call it the "off-beat shuffle," and it swings like a dog! The first time I heard it was by Jabo Starks; he had a tune out called "I Don't Need Me No Woman." I think it was on Mercury.

T.G.: Also I noticed right away that it hooks up with a common rhythm guitar pattern where they chunk on all the upbeats. When you lock in with the rhythm guitar like that it really adds power to the groove.

M.C.: It creates an incredible driving force. Years ago, if for some reason there was no guitar player on the gig we would play it to compensate for their rhythm part.

It's an important part of the history of the music, and I learned it with everything else that came along. It's really effective at a medium tempo. Another thing that I'll say here is that when I play this I hold the sticks so that I catch part of the rim and get that "clang" that's got a bite to it.

T.G.: A characteristic of this particular shuffle is that there are no strong two and four backbeats. If you were going to play something like "Let the Good Times Roll" that calls for that driving backbeat, you wouldn't choose this shuffle. On the other hand, in the proper context, it's not necessary to have that backbeat because it's providing such a forward propelling rhythm. It drives the beat in its own powerful way.

M.C.: Indeed. It's a loose limb activity.

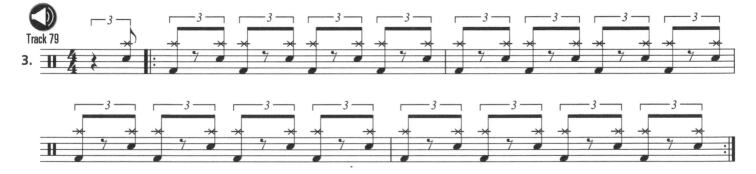

M.C.: Here's a pattern that works well with an organ player. With this one, you're playing the back half of the shuffle with the left hand and the other half with the bass drum. You can really lay back on the snare. It's perfect for a kind of lazy tempo. I usually play a jazz ride beat with this one, rather than a shuffle ride. It creates a really nice loping feeling that kind of takes care of itself.

T.G.: You put it on cruise control.

M.C.: Yeah, there's not a lot of thinking involved (which is a good thing!). It gets the job done.

T.G.: What is it about this groove that makes it useful when playing with an organ player?

M.C.: Well, the organ bass is thick and not as clean as the electric bass. It has more sustain. Playing the shuffle this way helps the rhythm cut through. You can feel the rhythm better with the snare and bass drum alternating back and forth. You can play a kind of lazy feel and it will hold the time together.

This one can be effective for fast tempos. Experiment and find an appropriate tune.

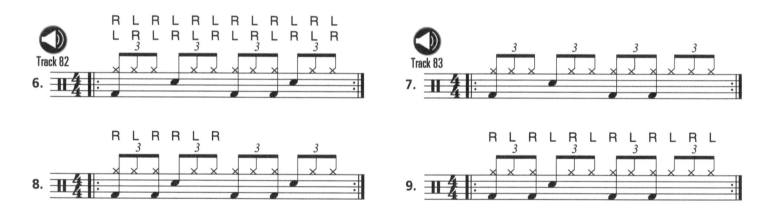

T.G.: Here we have the double shuffle played with an accent on all the upbeats like the previous one.

M.C.: It's the same feel, but with the double shuffle underneath it. Some blues bands would play a real fast break tune, and you could use this for that kind of thing.

Slow Blues

T.G.: Now, we have the infamous Mike Clark slow blues.

M.C.: This is another Ray Torres special, although I've taken it and done something else with it—made it my own. Ray was the first guy I heard play a slow blues this way. He was playing the standard 12/8 rhythm but filled it in with ghost sixteenth notes here and there. This gave it a tambourine-like effect. When you listened out in front of the bandstand with the whole band playing, it gave a real gospel church sound to the music.

Being that I'd been on about a billion organ gigs, he showed it to me. As the years went by, I just kept creating variations of the original beat in a multitude of different ways. The syncopation in the bass drum can give you a very funky feel.

Sometimes I'll play this groove throughout an entire tune. Other times, I'll just use it to change the feel from one section to another—maybe behind a solo. It really is one of those grooves that propels the music, and it's highly effective when used at the appropriate time. I wouldn't recommend using it every time you play a slow blues, as this could diminish its effectiveness. You'll figure out where to use it through experimentation and experience.

T.G.: I noticed that here you are using the same idea as in the Breakdown section, where the hands are floating or idling over the top, and the bass drum carries the accents, punctuation, and syncopation.

And here again, you continue to vary the syncopation over an extended part of the tune. To me this creates a sense of intrigue and mystery, yet never loses the listener as they follow intently along. It makes the music more interesting.

M.C.: Yes, Paul Jackson refers to it as "talkin' with the bass drum."

Talking with the Bass Drum:

Track 88

Song Excerpts

From the Herbie Hancock album *Thrust*

"Actual Proof"

This piece was a milestone in my career. It became quite famous, and I was credited with a drumming innovation as a result. Incorporating one of my original funk grooves and borrowing heavily from jazz vocabulary as an undercurrent, I created a running commentary weaving throughout the narrative of the song, making observations, statements, and comments on what Herbie was playing during his solo. This is the most interesting and exciting way to play, allowing and facilitating an open dialogue between the musicians. By that I mean open, interactive, and conversational, as opposed to straight-time drumming, where you are relegated to playing fills now and then.

T.G.: You have an uncanny knack for syncopated displacement of the open hi-hat. How did you develop that?

M.C.: I wasn't intentionally trying to be tricky, but that's just the way I hear it. I open and close the hi-hat in places where most people don't. I used it as a way to put a different twist on things, and it became part of my style. I found it more interesting than the more obvious places to open the hi-hat.

"Palm Grease"

For "Palm Grease" and "Spank-A-Lee," Herbie asked me to come up with more of a pocket-oriented, less expansive type of groove—not as complex as the playing on "Actual Proof." So I used a two-measure groove that I felt was good and funky, yet more interesting than the usual two and four backbeat.

"Spank-A-Lee"

"Spank-A-Lee"

For "Spank-A-Lee" I used a typical Oakland-type feel from that time period. It's an extremely syncopated sixteenth-note groove with a recurring hi-hat jazz ride pattern that I stole from Dave Garibaldi.

From the Mike Clark album *Actual Proof*

"Aristide"

For "Aristide," I borrowed a piece of a famous Bernard Purdie beat. I played a backward jazz ride hi-hat with a funk underlay and kept the beat loose and open so there'd be plenty of room to stretch out during the solos.

Variations

Without open hi hat

"Stingers"

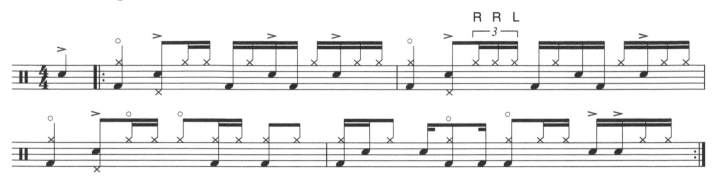

"The Grinder"

T.G.: On your album *Actual Proof* you recorded a tune called "The Grinder." It is a sixteenth-note feel with a lot of bass drum in the pattern. How did you come up with this beat?

M.C.: One of my drum heroes is Ray Torres, a dear friend and a great drummer. He always put the bass drum accent on the "and" of the beat, on the upbeat instead of the downbeat. I loved how he made the band feel when he did that, so I added that to my thing, and "The Grinder" is a take-off on his rhythm. He played this beat back in 1963. This is my adaptation of it, and over time I expanded on it and made it my own.

From *Return of the Headhunters*

"Tip Toe Through the Ghetto"

On "Tip Toe," I came up with an idea where the punctuation falls on the last sixteenth note of beats 2 and 4 as the primary pulse. Then I would just sprinkle the hi-hat and snare drum in between them to hold it together.

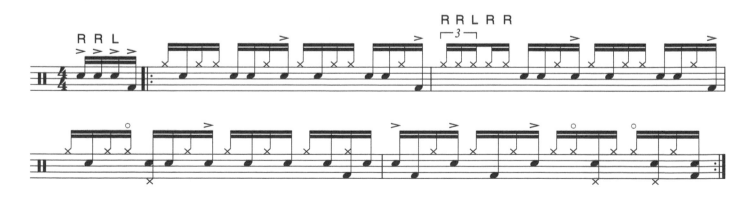

From the Headhunters Album *Evolution/Revolution*

"Loft Funk"

This is another one of my linear grooves. I use a match grip and cross the right hand over the top of the left to play the hi-hat. I got this hand movement from Frank Katz, a truly great, original drummer. I wrote this tune along with saxophone great Jed Levy for the Headhunter album *Evolution/Revolution*.

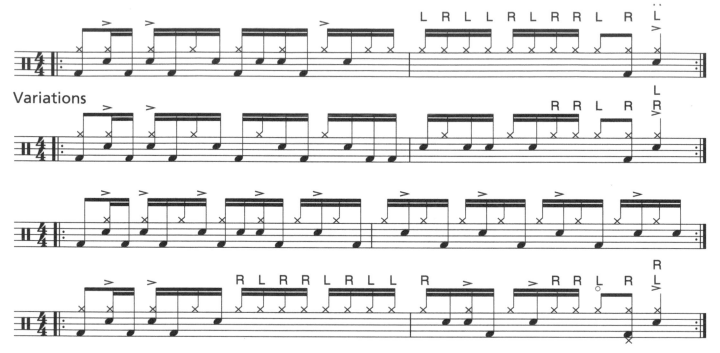

Variations

"Evolution/Revolution"

T.G.: This song represents your most recent work, as of this writing (Oct. 2003). When I listened to this track, I was most intrigued by the fact that it seemed to cover the entire spectrum of music—from the Afro-Cuban rhythms that are a continuation of African rhythms played for at least several hundred years, to the most modern funk grooves. Gerry Gonzales and the Fort Apache Band have also been very successful in blending roots music with the most modern jazz elements.

Drum Interlude

From the Mike Clark album *The Funk Stops Here*

"Four String Drive"

On "Four String Drive" and "Slinky" I played linear grooves (see Linear Grooves chapter). This is a distinct concept from coordinated independence, where the hands and feet work against each other.

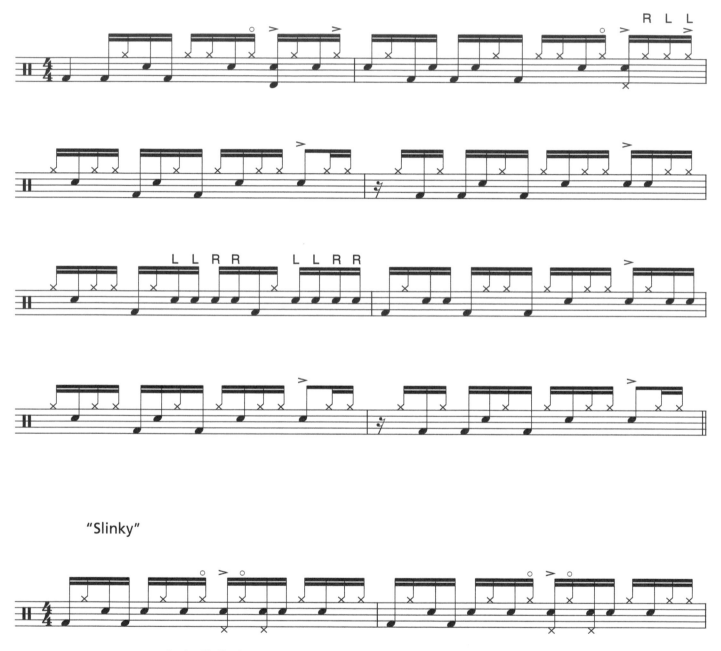

"Slinky"

Here are two more of my favorites from *The Funk Stops Here* thrown in for good measure.

"Swamp Thing"

"Spiderman"

*Sometimes I close the hi-hat on the "e" of the beat instead of the "and."

Respect and Gratitude

Ray Torres

Although a few other drummers have been credited with inventing the sixteenth-note funk style, the first time I ever heard it was from a drummer named Ray Torres in 1967 in Fort Worth, Texas. "Good Rockin' Ray" had the most unique sense of rhythm; he played over the bar and in between the beats while the band played on top of it. He almost never ended a phrase on beat 1. You never knew what to expect, except that whatever he did, it had to be funky. He was called "Good Rockin' Ray" for a reason. The man could rock you down.

I used to get out of my car, and you always knew he was playing because you could feel the ground rocking in the parking lot! He'd put extra spice on all the notes, as if he were making a stew—stirring and adding flavor until he got it just right. He could shade and color rolls and fills that would make you stop what you were doing and tilt your head sideways—listening carefully like the RCA dog. I never heard him copy anyone; he was truly a very different drummer with his own individual take on things. He had such a nasty Texas shuffle and could get so funky that even non-musicians would leave the club talking about him. Everybody knew.

Ray took time out to train me and show me his style. He is my dear friend and brother, and I owe my success directly to him for planting the seed of funk deep in my soul.

Bernard "Pretty" Purdie

The first time I heard Bernard Purdie was on King Curtis's record *Live at the Fillmore West*. The track was called "Memphis Soul Stew." When King Curtis yelled, "Gimme a half a pound of fatback drums!!" and Bernard came in with that beat, I almost passed out. That groove changed the history of funk drumming forever. That groove brought to the forefront the ghost note (or sixteenth-note) drum style and allowed drummers, such as myself, to have great careers. I still use that groove today, and it sounds timeless—as modern today as it did when I first heard it in 1971.

His signature hi-hat lick that all of us use is one of the most important innovations in drumming history. Bernard is a genius of rhythm, funk, and soul for whom I have much love and gratitude. Thank you, Bernard "Pretty" Purdie so very much!

Clyde Stubblefield

I feel that all drummers playing today's music owe Clyde Stubblefield a profound debt of gratitude. Personally, without his enormous contribution, I would not have been able to play the things I did on "Actual Proof." This is a track that brought me fame and honors in the drumming community that keep coming in to this very day. What he did on *James Brown Sex Machine Live in Augusta* (especially the songs "Give It Up" and "Turn It Loose") paved the way for all modern drumming. That's the funkiest groove I have ever heard since being on the planet, and I think I have heard them all and played a few myself. Thank you Clyde!

Jabo Starks

Jabo Starks played one of the finest shuffles I've ever heard. He had such a deep and soulful feeling, and it came through in everything I heard him play. Check out the off-beat shuffle he plays on Bobby Blue Bland's "I Don't Want No Woman." Too cold, Jabo.

David Garibaldi

David Garibaldi took the funk thing in another direction, adding his personal point of view to everything he did. He was one of the great innovators who got people interested in playing funk music, Oakland style. I love all of Garibaldi's inventions and creativity. As soon as Tower of Power hit the scene, all the musicians wanted to play the funky stuff.

Gaylord Birch

Unfortunately, Gaylord passed away. He was a fierce Oakland funk drummer with a jazz intellect. A tremendously charismatic performer, he possessed a powerful spirit that raised the music to an incredible level of excitement. He played and recorded with The Pointer Sisters, Cold Blood, Graham Central Station, Bobby Hutcherson, Charles Brown, Bonnie Raitt, and many other jazz and funk groups.

Elvin Jones

The impact Elvin Jones has had on contemporary drum style is comparable to the role that Muhammad Ali played to all successive generations of boxers. After listening to Elvin, I learned how to totally immerse the rhythm into the musical conversation of the moment. As with all good dialogue, listening is as vital as expression if the communication is going to realize the fullest potential. From him, I learned to hear everything going on around me all the time—to choose to react or not react—enabling me to be more active and not relegated to simply keeping time. Elvin is the king of triplets. He utilized them as not just an occasional flourish but as a constant propulsion underpinning the current of the piece. At times, eighth notes or sixteenth notes can be stiff and restrict the flow, while playing triplets expedites more opportunities for improvisation among all the players and liberates the soloist. I cannot emphasize enough the profound influence he has had on my drumming and all of the current music we hear today.

Tony Williams

What can I say about Tony that hasn't been said already? The man was a genius. What he did changed the course of drumming forever. He was the first drummer I ever heard to combine jazz and rock the way he did. His fiery cymbal work coupled with his insane polyrhythmic executions mesmerized and baffled generations of drummers. Many people have since based their careers on playing Tony Williams's musical afterthoughts. He has personally had the strongest influence on me of any drummer who has ever lived. From the Miles period to the post-Miles era, he always expanded on and demonstrated a level of drumming and musicality of exquisite skill. Tony taught me the spirit of challenging one's self, physically, spiritually, and mentally. He was a true visionary and teacher.

Lenny White

I first heard Lenny White in the early seventies on Freddie Hubbard's *Red Clay*. He sounded to me like a combination of Elvin Jones and Tony Williams. I was completely impressed. I later heard him live with Joe Henderson and Woody Shaw. He became a major influence on me. He had one of the deepest, nastiest ride beats I had ever heard. I always tell my students if they want to learn how to swing, they need to go to one of his gigs and sit under his ride cymbal. His playing on *Bitches Brew* was pioneering groundwork for what came to be known as fusion. His jagged and purposely displaced phrasing reflects his innate understanding of jazz language. This instinct enables him to constantly push the envelope and play without a net, so to speak. My interpretation of his work, as well as the lessons I learned from Tony Williams and Elvin Jones, influenced my own contribution when I played "Actual Proof" with Herbie Hancock on *Thrust*. Lenny's work with Chick Corea's Return to Forever and his later solo projects elaborated on the developing jazz rock language and opened the door for all who followed. One of my true drum heroes, Lenny is truly a major innovator on the instrument.

Discography

As a Leader

Summertime	JazzKey Records
Actual Proof	Platform
Mike Clark—The Headhunter	Ubiquity
The Funk Stops Here	Enja
New York Funk	Grammavision
Give the Drummer Some	Stash

With the Headhunters

Straight from the Gate	Arista
Survival of the Fittest	Arista
Evolution/Revolution	Basin Street Records
Return of the Headhunters	Verve

As a Sideman

Thrust (Herbie Hancock)	Columbia
Manchild (Herbie Hancock)	Columbia
Flood (Herbie Hancock)	Columbia
Deathwish (Herbie Hancock)	Columbia
Herbie Hancock's Greatest Hits	Columbia
Herbie Hancock Boxed Set	CBS/Sony
Charlie Brown Christmas Special (Vince Guaraldi)	Fantasy
Do They Hurt? (Brand X)	Passport
Product (Brand X)	Passport
Alien Army (Jack Wilkins)	Music Masters
They Call Him Reckless (Jack Wilkins)	Music Masters
Revenge of the Fat People	Stash
Heritage (Eddie Henderson)	Blue Note
They Say I'm Different (Betty Davis)	Columbia
The Hunter (Henry Franklin)	Resurgent Music
The Shade (Mark Puricelli)	Music Masters
Melting Point (Mark Puricelli)	Music Masters
Blues and the Abstract Truth (Suzanne Pittson)	Vineland
At Home on the Road (Harvey Wainapple)	Jazz Mission
The One Mind Experience (Bishop Norman Williams)	Theresa
The Raven (Dave Ellis)	Milestones

Videos

Rhythm Combinations (Mike Clark & Paul Jackson)	Rittor Music
Funky Drummers (Mike Clark, Dennis Chambers, Dave Garibaldi & Chad Smith)	DCI

Epilogue

I hope this book helped many of you aspiring funkateers to unlock some of my personal secrets in the art of funk drumming, as well as give you insight into some of the great geniuses that invented and influenced it. I can't name them all, but to get an idea of where some of the funk came from, please check out Robert Johnson, Guitar Slim, Howlin' Wolf, Hubert Sumlin, Albert King, Freddy King, B.B. King, Albert Collins, Big Mama Thornton, Laverne Baker, Roy Brown, Wynonie Harris, Roscoe Gordon, Bobby Rush, Ruth Brown, Louis Jordan, Big Maybelle, Otis Redding, Sam and Dave, the Bar-Kays, the Marquees, Otis Rush, Little Milton Campbell, Bobby Blue Bland, James Brown, Little Richard, Bobby Marchan, Ike and Tina Turner, Robert Parker, Little Junior Parker, Little Willie John, Jr. Walker, Muddy Waters, Slim Harpo, John Lee Hooker, Sonny Boy Williamson, Junior Wells, Buddy Guy, Lowell Folsom, the Neville Brothers, Ernie K. Doe, Magic Sam, Little Walter Jacobs, Big Walter Horton, Etta James, Otis Spann, Jimmy Reed, James Cotton, Jesse Hill, the Temptations, Smokey Robinson and the Miracles, Ray Charles, the Isley Brothers, Fred Wesley, the JBs, Bobby Hebb, Sly and the Family Stone, Tower of Power, Graham Central Station, Watts 103rd Street Band, the Ohio Players, Marvin Gaye, the Marvellettes, Jackie Wilson, Dee Clark, Shorty Long, Edwin Starr, Gatemouth Brown, Lee Dorsey, Joe Jones, Little Esther, Candy Staton, Aretha Franklin, Gladys Knight and the Pips, Rufus and Carla Thomas, Irma Thomas, Betty Wright, Little Eva, Doris Troy, Big Jay McNeely, Bill Doggett, Frankie Ford, Fats Domino, the Coasters, the Olympics, Wilson Pickett, Johnny Copeland, Dr. John, Lloyd Price, Bobby Darin, Ramsey Lewis, Eddie Harris, Les McCann, and let's not forget Herbie Hancock and the Headhunters. If that don't get you, nothing will!

Track 89 Closing Groove

"The Breakdown"

Special Thanks

Special thanks to Linda Reynolds for her creative input and copyediting skills. Towner Galaher is a great drummer and composer, whose friendship, astute musicianship, and collaboration inspired and guided this book from beginning to end.

Towner Galaher

A native of the Pacific Northwest, Towner Galaher moved to New York City in 1986. He has studied Afro-Caribbean drumming with Frankie Malabe, Johnny Almendra, Bobby Sanabria, and Victor Rendon, Brazilian drumming with Duduka Fonseca and Cyril Baptiste, New Orleans drumming with Ricky Sebastian, and jazz and funk drumming with Mel Brown and Mike Clark.

With a vast array of experience working in such diverse styles as musical theater, country, jazz, blues, R&B, funk, New Orleans R&B, marching, and Latin bands, Towner has performed with some of the top names in jazz, including Wynton Marsalis, John Faddis, Jon Hendricks, Arvel Shaw (Louis Armstrong), guitar legend Jack Wilkins, and Arturo O'Farrill, leader of Chico O'Farill's Afro-Cuban Big Band.

A bandleader, composer, and arranger, his dynamic new ensemble is a frequent fixture on the local jazz club circuit and was featured at the inaugural Astoria-Long Island City Jazz Festival. *Panorama*, his recently released CD, features five original compositions plus three jazz standards and a stellar lineup of musicians: Charles Fambrough on bass, Onaje Allen Gumbs on piano, Maurice Brown on trumpet, Mark Shim on tenor, as well as master percussionists Frank Colon and Johnny Almendra.

Towner holds a BA in music from Empire State College, an MA in jazz performance from Queens College, and is the author of three seminal essays, "Parallel Developments and Cross-Cultural Exchange in the Music of Cuba and New Orleans 1900–1920," "The History of Latin Music in New York City," and "New Orleans R&B 1945–1970." As an educator, he has worked in New York City's public school system, local community centers, and maintains a thriving private teaching practice.

His drumming book *Coordination Development for the Drum Set* will prepare the student to play the syncopated and independent rhythms in *Funk Drumming* as well as all Latin, jazz, and funk drumming. Visit www.townergalahermusic.com for more information.